T0329057

Shades of Black

Poetry

Edward Dzonze

Edited by Tendai Rinos Mwanaka

Mwanaka Media and Publishing Pvt Ltd,
Chitungwiza Zimbabwe
*
Creativity, Wisdom and Beauty

Publisher:
Mwanaka Media and Publishing Pvt Ltd *(Mmap)*
24 Svosve Road, Zengeza 1
Chitungwiza Zimbabwe
mwanaka@yahoo.com
mwanaka13@gmail.com
www.africanbookscollective.com/publishers/mwanaka-media-and-publishing
https://facebook.com/MwanakaMediaAndPublishing/

Distributed in and outside N. America by African Books Collective
orders@africanbookscollective.com
www.africanbookscollective.com

ISBN: 978-1-77929-594-1
EAN: 9781779295941

DISCLAIMER
All views expressed in this publication are those of the author and do not
necessarily reflect the views of *Mmap*.

Dedication

To *Kupakwashe Farai* Dzonze and *Stacey Hannah* Dzonze-
These are the words taught to me by your absence.
This here is the coffee we share with the African world
To *Edzaisu* Trust and Action Hub creatives, Nyasha Charakupa and
Admire Matema the IrieMan;
We were together in this lyrical making
To Dr. Tanaka Chidora and the Poetry Intercourse Family-
Gugulethu Garwe, my pillar of strength .
Here is to you Mr & Mrs F.Dzonze, the same goes to Nation Godzi
and Wellington Matangi
These are the songs we sang together
And of course the publisher who made it happen

Table of Contents :

Foreword

Art is a garment that refuses to be defined by a person's figure. Every Artist speaks from where he stands and the same garment looks completely different. My art is about how I live and perceive, how everything around me makes me believe. The burden of an Artist is to articulate. The clock ticks, the drama unfolds..., here the artist is called to capture. The pastor preach, the congregates bleach...., here the artist is called to question. When the people speak and the superiors they speak to, take a dive deep into the corruption pools the people speak to question, here the artist is called to sing. When the sun denies us the lustre at anticipated times, when the moon submits to darkness before we see the road awaiting us...we paint the pictures to depict the terrain and ask a question or plenty. When the land we have cannot make a home for us....

If you are speculating from an African vantage point, you know it's the Black Coffee awaiting the African fella for breakfast tomorrow. Those are the Shades of Black for you...

Black Coffee

Without a grain of sugar,
No drop of milk whatsoever
Black coffee is served as compliment to our black skin
Black coffee served by a black Chef
Proclaiming it in a language known to his kith and kin-
This black coffee is all the black pot can offer for breakfast
Take a sip or take a swim ,black coffee is good for your melanin
Verily so, the black coffee depicts the taste of life in the African
ghetto

Without a grain of sugar
No drop of milk whatsoever-
The black coffee is served plain
We sip to conform to what comes with their political reign-
Throwing bombs in every path we tread,
Discolouring the African flag with blood stains
I speak of rivers of blood because the gore is what's flowing in the
African streets
They serve the coffee with pride
They have got guns to show us to the coffee mugs
The sight of those guns reminding us to enjoy the ride in quietude
Verily so, the black coffee depict the taste of life in the African
ghetto

Without a grain of sugar
No drop of milk whatsoever ,
Even the Chef who serve the coffee doesn't dare to take a sip
It's them who know how the milk and honey tastes
They've got the keys to the diamond fields
Their life is a sparkle, they live a life on our behalf
Because the black pot knows only their palms

And it is never their children who drinks what they serve
We sip to conform to what comes with their political reign
Verily so, the black coffee depicts the taste of life in the African
ghetto

The Geek before the Mirror

There goes the geek
Word is the jungle,
The geek is the beat of the jungle
It takes only him and his shadow to tango
Lyrically this here is how he winks
His wit stinks on poetry pages
But that smell is right to the flow of the clock
Shouting obscenities to the nakedness of life
Spitting rhymes to rebuke the sting of bitter days
Wandering the Hararean mazes in torn pants shadowing the might of
his writing pen
To live is to write, he writes to observe whats on the right side of
verse
Sleeping only when tabloids turn the stink of his wit
Into music, precisely the chorus to the dark shades of his passion

Desperate Virgins

When the clouds above
Promise the nation no drop of rain
Our sense of belonging summons us to weep
Irrigating the African flower with our tears thus
Desperate virgins pledging their virginity to negotiate a desired
serenity
Sleeping around with the predators who calls them prostitutes
Because the pennies they folk out for the desperate virgins makes
their families smile
Because they verily know how the once virgins
 Lost their virginity in a quest to live the day before they dream again
of the days to come
The desperate virgins pulls down their knickers to rise above shame

When the gold in our hands cannot make our lives golden
When the rubies and diamonds we have cannot enrich our
livelihoods
When all the land we have cannot make a home for us to live
When the wind blowing on our turf cannot give us an air to breathe
When the sum total of the black we live fail to amount to the black
we are
When the sacrosanct altar the freedom fighters took a bullet to
protect
Lay in shame in the wake of our miseries,
Starring at us, starring at our livelihoods flow in the same shame
When the breasts to suckle the newly born drips venom instead of
milk
The desperate virgins go with the call of prostitutes

We flood the streets with our tears
The life we live in the African streets is far from sweet

We flood the African parliament with the same tears
But the African legislators enjoy swimming for a political hobby
When we cry too loud for the neighbours to bring a wise counsel
They flood the streets with the blood of unsuspecting citizens
Depriving them of an entitled freedom
We roam still as desperate virgins
But those who verily know the predicament to our chastity call us by
the names we despise
Makwerekwere points to the height of our desperation
Grigamba, Botsotso is what they called me in Namibia
Prostitutes is what they called our desperate mothers in Kuwait
While the fathers were shown another man's arse to kiss as gate pass
to the day's morsel
We roam still, gunshots come as an endnote to the flow of our
livelihoods
We roam still,
They have different names for us other than immigrants
We roam still, the tattered rags we wear for clothes
Make us look the virgins we try to live

Broken Guitar: Fare thee well

Oliver

The legend is gone, his day is done

What to say and do,

When the guitar strings we danced to yesterday

woke up consumed by the providence of fate

The cruel storm blew away the rhythms and melodies
we had grown accustomed to

Sparking a cry that culminated into this lyrical articulation

We smiled and danced when he rose to churn

We danced together with Oliver,

we danced along to his penned verses

We danced to embrace the musical touch our ears refused to resist

The world is in tears, our beloved Tuku is gone

We lived with the guru
and learnt the humble ways of life from his guitar strings ,

The rhythms of his African drum
teaching us to take pride of our being

Sweet melodies reaching out to the world in pain

He had on his guitar, a string that knew how to heal a wounded heart

When he rose to sing, he took away a tear from the face of the troubled,

dissolving it in the musical magic borne of his mind and fingers

Oliver did that with his musical embrace

He taught us to dance a dance we shall forever dance

For his genius lives justifiably amongst all...

We cursed the sunset for biting us where it hurts

You were the sun that conquered darkness

through dulcets, the heartbeat of your guitar

You showed us the good from the bad

You were a flower that decorated our minds with profound wisdom,

Today we smile, you breathed eternity at Pakare Paye

Look, me and Selmor today boasts of a haven for a home

Fare thee well beloved Oliver

we shall live with the voice, the melodies will show us the light

From your musical spell, our hearts remember how you turned everything sour into a danceable melody

For we shall live to take solace from the wise counsel of your flute

You breathed life into the world of many

I wish i could just hum the songs you sang

I remember now this song you sang ;
Rufu ndimadzongonyedze...

Fare thee well musical Doctor
Tingaiteko vatonga

Mourning The Fall of The Antidote; Elegy to a Musical Icon

Life is forever getting sour in our hearts

Yesterday we mourned the fall of a giant,

We mourned *Mtukudzi* the legend who gave us the desired shape of a
guitar

That was only yesterday...

How to say it so you feel it is the burden

Before that tear could dry away from our faces

We wake up to the devastating news of *Mungoshi's* departure

Where is death taking our heroes to?

We mourn the fall of our giants
when death comes to harvest the flowers we cherish ,

The flowers that beautifies our garden, mother earth

Without the antidote, sour gets even sourer

We shall live with the pain, our beloved Antidote is gone

She is gone, the dearest is gone,
That vibrant voice that travelled the span of earth
to ignite a light that forever shines

She gave us melodies, the kind that finds its own way to the heart

With her guitar she painted the face of this world in humanity colours,

She gave us a melody and we all rose to dance

She gave us a vibe, the vibes that comes with light as a shadow,

The light that illuminates the dark corridors of survival

Many were the songs we danced to

I am afraid this space is too small to suffice the weight,

I would rather play the harp or a flute

While the silence of her absence vocalize to the same

She, the Hero who breathed fire to the justification of women existence along the masculine , not just as companion but as beings alike

She, the chanter who got us all enchanted in the sweetness of music

We shall live with the pain

For today the antidote has departed this earth

We mourn the fall of our giants
Her day is done, Auntie Dot has departed this world

Gone from our faces,

She continues to live with us in those guitar strings

Let the music we all danced to remind us to celebrate her worthy life

and bid farewell thus to our beloved

Rest in purpose dearest

Rest in peace beloved Dorothy
Here is to the antidote that heal

Here We Stand

Indepedence was the genesis

This lyrical testimony a revation
Of how politics became our nemesis

And then dear mother's breast dripped vernom instead of milk

when the saints became evil,
The demons assume the angels

And barbarity reigns,

Nobody is ashamed to carry a blood stain before the parliament

Freedom is not a gain when corruption is permitted a flow

Black barbaric brethrens baptized in the brutality of their blood
stinking ideogies

Playing audience to the demise of everything sensible

I hate that the black of my skin carries the shame

Gunshots to silence the streets from protest

See them cheer and smile to see the denizen
Bowing to a Holy Communion of their barbarity

Prospects of change
Rolled on ballot paper for the judiciary to puff

And declare the joke legitimate after elections

Of course the electorate chokes

But there is the consolotion of tear gas

For rioters who dispute the judiciary's billow

For what they know, not what is fed unto them by the might of politics

New binds upon our livelihoods,

The black Gods reing over hell
For their justification of black freedom

What matters to them is the establishment of a black kingdom

Where black slaves are content with the illusionary tag of "Kings" on their slave jackets

To convince them this hell is a black spell

Where the stink of freedom will turn into a pleasant smell
When politics turn up with a key to their cell

Africa on the zoom
Politicians dating the game for riches and fame

To us the gain is this shame

A ragged flag to proclaim the degree of our emancipation

The freedom that exists in the songs we sing-

How Nkrumah and Mugabe yearned for it

In the cold embrace of apartheid and imperialism

Steve Biko taking a bullet to set a country free

Mandela submitting his hands for the price of freedom

What with Amilcar Cabral knocking for that freedom to his death bed

Freedom is a shame when politicians
Strip naked its essence, bedding the significance thereof

To concieve this penury and bloodshed for us to learn a thing about governance,

reminding the children of revolutionaries what their fathers fought for,

Why the streets are named after them
In the wake of it all, spelling it unto all that its not them to blame

Animal Farm: A tale of Hyenas and the Sheep

There is a cross, a hammer and the nails
The train is going off the rail, a piece of truth here served in braille
Everybody sheds a tear for evil to sail
The hammer looks certain to descend on the nails
When the freedom flag bleed its him
Welcome to Hell, the heaven of our tormentors
Every mansion is a jail cell
The air we breathe is verily stale
How the devil rose is how the nation fell
Outside the prison cell people live in a shell
Where their breath is the will of the serpent
Poli-(tick)-ing goes with the tock of the clock
There is no shepherd, there is no flock
Unless the hyenas chose to assume the monk in a brothel
Where the sheep is a raunchy whore
Him the devil, fondles the breast of the gods at night
Forces his black head between the thighs of a nation in labour
The wrath and anguish of the gods comes to his favour
You should hear the hyenas laugh
When the pasture runs dry
Its manna to them when the livestock starve to death

House of Hunger

Freedom wreaks when the foul mouthed speaks
      The dark clouds above points to a sour rain

The African flag turned against its say
      When an impoverished soldier

Opens fire to speak the political mind of the might
      A ball of fire to the famished denizens

It all dissolves with the rain of the iron fist

Beheaded dreams and castrated thoughts
      Hope is a colony of how they reign

Decapitated to just roam in the dirt and mirk of it
      Everybody is a parcel awaiting delivery in this jungle

Governance all the missing part of the puzzle
      Entittled freedoms driping from the spout of the muzzle

Corruption a revelation to their evolution
      Take a bow to milk the cannonized cows
Everything clearly spelled with their reign, this is how

One hopes the country will mend
      While the other hops to where a country is spent

This country is surely dead

Only the phantom of it gives ground to dreamers

One takes a bomb for defying the tomb
    While the other gets a doctarate for curing the ailment that
consumed a nation to bleak

This country is surely diseased
    Only the disease is what motions the flow of everything

What of democracy in the wake of it all,
    Fuck the dictates, they wear it like a condom

To ease the going till they reach the orgasm
    Used condoms all around their governance
They have their ego protected against the peoples grievances

See the still shadows of our sacrosanct bleeding walls
    Frown to dispell the stink of a sour rain

Bread beyond the price of food, this is how
    Meat beyond the price of relish, just the how

Sugar beyond the price of sweet, this is how
    Bullets and guns moderating the people's grieviances
beyond mumbling and whispering,this is how

Gambling is all the offer on the job market, this is how
One hopes change will come with the morning sun

Yet change is what the guns stands against....
    This is how they spell a civilisation

Hoisting the freedom flag while an anthem plays to proclaim it to the world.
    This is our taste of freedom...
They seem a people from a distant
    It's safe to say when their ego points to the opposite direction, this here is how

Rivers Running Dry

When the rivers we have known
  To deliver the waters of   survival run dry
    The gods that watch over the spout summon our tears and
      blood to a sanctioned flow
    The scars on my face
Is clear testament of the bloody games we play in Africa,
          The bloody games we play to fool the spectator
          Those who die are mere rotten apples
          They have seen many perish in war
          What they have now is a country to run
        And besides, what's the value of a rotten apple
      When you know how a fresh one tastes
    Dust to dust as we mourn the departed
  But the guns i see in town
Are loaded to spark another cloud of the same dust

Gunshots in Mogadishu, cry my beloved Maiduguri
  For your children cannot quench their thirst
    With the political pee of extremist Jihadists
      Whose barbarity continue to deprive the human worth of
      the abductees
        Streams of tears and blood meandering and
        crisscrossing the African turf
        Do not mistake the gunshots in Harare for a familiar
        drumbeat
        Cry for your children my beloved Africa
    Addis Ababa cannot sleep a peaceful sleep with these guns
parroting madness for a song
    While a political flame is burning the African flag

When the rivers we have known to deliver

The waters of survival run dry
The gods who watch over the spout summon our tears and
blood to a sanctioned flow
Rat tat tat , boom! ...the sound of the blast
Those expensive guns in town
Will only write anew the story of poverty upon
the African turf
Shame, they will watch a sister strip naked
to show them a naked boob
Before they toss a coin for her to show them
the sanctuary
How are we to cross the bridge when we dress
the children with military camouflage
Give them weapons to kill before telling them the
African is not a brother when his name is not known to you- rotten
apple
Indeed the guns will instill fear among the citizens
Their politics will reign, the blood stain doesn't appear
on their Gucci pants
Remember they have a country to run
And besides, mind where you tread
You just do not want to look the rotten apple before their
thirsty guns

Orphans of His Legendry

I am as high as a cloud
All my troubles beneath me
I shake my spears from the cockpit
The sting of my tongue tearing through like the sun's rays
Now that the reader is basking in The Black Sunlight
I am tempted to book the next flight to deliver the meal to the
galleries
Where readers roam in tears for what their wit cant miss on
poetry pages
Draging Marechera's name through the stink of my flow
To churn the songs that resonate with their known taste
of verse
Our wit coincide on a gem that shines equally bright in our
eyes
One splash of ink
To get the reader inclined to the exegesis to the genesis of verse
High is where i am taking this verse
The first line falls within the context of the law
And for those who miss the legend of verse, here is how
i'm checking in to say hello .

Guns And Bulldozers

(I am writing to shame the ugly things that have come to haunt the Black of my skin)

Rat tat tat tat,
  watch where you tread
They have got bullets loaded   in their AKz
     Rat tat tat tat
The world is in trouble with the sound of the gun
       They make the jungle rumble in a stampede of panic
        Rat tat tat tat tat
Wake up from yesteryear slumber if you still identify that sound from
a familiar movie
    The African government wants the people to grieve with a smile
      So they look the government
they want the people to believe
Rat tat tat tat
The world is in trouble with the sound of the gun i tell you my friend
     Nobody wants that for a soundtrack

They've got tear gases
to   choke the streets for asking
questions they don't have answers to,
     They will have button sticks to our buttocks
If we don't jump up to the sound of their treasured guns
     They've got shields to cover up their masked faces
     Even the law is too low for the heights of their politicized
madness
     They've got loaded AKz to silence activists
     Just do not look for justice in this plot
     The police got cuffs to seal the trinity of the stinking
ploy

What does it matter to say a thing to them,
they will have the situation under control
       Commiserations to us all, the uniformed masked fella
don't have a name
       The lost blood is on the uniform and in no man's hands
       Like so, the government regrets any inconvenience

They clad our brothers with animosity,
gave them weapons and turned them against their fathers
      Watch where you tread, they got bullets loaded in their AKz
        Rat tat tat tat
the world is in trouble my friend
They use the microphone to preach the gospel of peace by day,
    only to resort to the muzzle when they want to whisper what their
political ego desires
They make the jungle rumble in a stampede of panic
   Do not ask the military for the political colour of their uniforms
You won't like it when thy open the muzzle to give you an answer
They serve us the Holy Communion of fear from an idling bulldozer
    Move, it's their world
The world is in trouble with the sound of a gun
        Nobody wants that for a soundtrack

(The keys to the poem are beneath the tittle
If you think you can turn off the terrifying bulldozer,)

Heart of a Woman

She is a flower that forever blooms
To every sun that comes to bless her living days
        She is the invisible sun
That shines inside the heart of every sensible man

The thief is her son,
The prostitute is her daughter
        She doesn't shy to tell you the truth you know;
'I suckled those two with the milk of my breast.'

It's the tears that accompanies the narration
    That tells you how much she despise their despicable
intransigence

        She buys candies and goodies
    Just to see the children smile until the candies claim a tooth
    I saw her defy the groom's order
    Not to give a crumb of the cake to a naughty boy
Who stuck out his leg when the groom was passing
        She took her share and gave it all to the naughty boy
Saying she only eats when the children are full
        She lied to her friends the other day
That she was fasting because there were just two buns for the three
of us
    Everything she buys with her money belongs to the family
        She tends the fields on rainy days
        She does so for the children and the lazy husband too,
Who loves her before taking the mug
        Only to kick and punch her after a calabash of homebrew

She has a heart like that;
She serenades the children with bedtime stories
That lulls them into a sweet sleep,
Waits on the couch for a drunk husband
   Who comes home without his waist, when a loving wife hungers
for intimate stories
Vomits on the bed and leave for a cheap mistress at the brothel
Who only calls him sweetheart when he has a beer in hand
   She keeps up with a man like that, calls him hubby still
   She beats up the children for disrespecting their father no matter
what
For all she cares, she want to raise her own sons to be sensible men
And her daughters to be phenomenal woman

Remembering Aunt Mucha

She once told me-
When you go hunting,

Do not let the benevolence of the wilderness
Entice you to consider the jungle for a home

The lions will come roaring after you,
    Saying the hyenas laughter is not good music for a hunter

What of stray lions that torments people in their own villages?

She smiled that smile of hers that would always culminate into a
chuckle,
            Eddie, what can you do about the wind unseen
That comes to blow away the sand beneath your feet?

I remember that smile of hers,
That would always culminate into a chuckle

I remember all her parables from that chuckle
    She once told me-
Not everyone who takes a dive
Makes it to the other side of the river

Some will drown, some will dive onto a sharp edged boulder beneath
the water
    With some becoming a meal for the crocodiles of the river
While some disappear mysteriously with the mermaids unseen

Even those who survive
Will survive to tell a tale of how they crossed the deadly river unhurt

I remember that unmistakable smile of hers,
That would always culminate into a chuckle

She smiled that smile of hers when she gave me a box of condoms
           Saying thus to me;
It's not every woman who hunts in the bar
Who gets a taste of the vile of promiscuity

Neither is there a woman in the church of God
Whose blood lives holier for the virus in her blood
               'Eddie, when you go out for a drink
And the drink goes beyond a sip, wear a condom'

She smiled, chuckled and began to cough
She gave me a nod, i kissed her cheek and left her bedside

I knew i might never see her smile again
I remember vividly the words she said when she gave me the red
ribbon;
        'It's not about the bloom of AIDS,
It's about the gloom, it's about the hope.'

Roaming Bird

The bird that flies away
To scavenge for food remembers its way back
to the nest,
The bird that follows the direction of the wind
Seek to take its wild dream to where the sky meets the
earth
The wind takes the bird to the mountains
Where the villagers knows best to trap roaming birds
The roaming bird finds itself a cage for a new home

A clever songbird sings from its nest,
It's the parroting that tethers a parrot to a fixed cage
The parrot imitates the seabird that sings of its rage
The roaming bird, now singing from a locked cage
Wish to fly to the next sky
Where the clouds will give a fresh breath of freedom
Getting to the next sky
The roaming bird will follow the direction of the new wind that
blows after slavery
It's what the caged bird sings,
It sings of a new wind of freedom-
A new wind to take her where the sky meets the earth

A roaming bird will follow the wind beyond the sea

She dreams of building her nest
Where the morning breeze will wake her up to a handful of
breadcrumbs,

She blames her own nest for the pouring rain
That shuttered its dry dream of a decorated sleep

She blames the nest she verily weaved
For the sunny days that comes with the shift of seasons

The roaming bird envies the weaver bird for its weaving dexterity
Her nest is not a home, she sings about it
She sings about the next sky, the reason Angelou knew why the
Caged Bird Sings
She will follow the wind to her wildest dreams
Where a morning breeze will wake her up to a handful of
breadcrumbs

She denounce her fixed cage in shrilled melodies
She dreams to fly again,
She wants the new sky to hear her singing
Yearning to get free so it roams to the new sky that exists in its
freedom quest

Raising The Verse

Writers speak to spark and ignite
The light that spans beyond their days on earth

We speak to spark the action
That speaks better of our collective actions and the regrettable lack
thereof

They recite to incite a worthy fight
That wins our desired ways over stupidity

We write to articulate and serve the collective wisdom
That lingers uncollected at the expedient behest of cultural
indoctrinations

We recite to shame how the people
Have embraced the passing wind blowing ashore their known values
and belief systems

They write to question the discourse of systems in the wake of
entitled freedoms
Even as they do so, they write to spark a light

Stick with the flow,
I have a loaded barrel
To take down the injustices undermining our entitled freedoms

Their Eyes Were Watching God, Zora Naele Hurston lives beyond
her days

She lives with us still, Angelou who Knows Why the Caged Bird
Sings

Chenjerai Hove's Red Hills of Home, the first verse that got me
nodding to poetry

Let the critic date the writer for his penmanship,

We speak to spark the action
That speaks better of our collective actions

I am not the first, i am not the last

I am the part of the verse that raises the same for the glorification of
the same

I have a date with an unknown reader
Who ordered for the verse of the day

It's not for me to say if this is the way
But if you can please follow the flow
I am called to honour the justice that calls in poetry

Ask me and i will tell you,
                            Writers speak to spark the action
That speaks better of our collective actions

Do not mistake the writer's position for what you can quote
    The writer poses as a mirror,
Reflecting to detail what is brought before its shiny surface

Never, the writer's pen doesn't bring the gagging smell onto a book
page
The writer's ink follows our stinking actions,
Expose them on book pages; the page becomes the dashboard

Those words you read are mere reflections
Those words seek to redirect us all in synch with the dynamics of the
day

I have a date with an unknown reader
Who has just ordered for the verse of the day

I have come to justify this verse among the galleries of verse
I want the reader to capture the flow, i want them to listen to the
songs
    I want them to identify their positions in the songs
Because all the songs are about them...
Their songs.

The Bloody Spear and The known Machete

The spear that killed my father
Did not come from a place unknown; it came from his brother's
hand
    The brother's killer silenced the grieving mourners with a
machete
He bought the casket, he bought thus our silence
  He remained with the bloody spear, we remained with the fear
      He shushed everyone to hear him weep
    He rinsed the blood on his spear with our tears
  We took solace from his condolences
You just don't wanna befriend his thirsty machete with tears on your
cheeks

They watch us grill on the embers of poverty,
That's what sparks their world

They swim in our miseries to enjoy the African sun

They cruise and glide on our sweat,

They skii and skate on our tears, it pleases them when we cry

But that costly pleasure is not enough for their political ego

What sparks their smile is seeing the African streets painted red with
human blood

We gave them a country to rule,
When the political spaceship rockets them to the sky

They take us all for a bowel of stool

Killing political activists when their guns are thirsty

They have got the money in plenty, everything falls on their side

They've got diamond fields in their vegetable gardens

I fail to see why our tears and blood have failed to choke their guilt

They don't sip the blood of the victims of their handgun with a golden straw
They use the blood to decorate their political dreams

Everybody knows the colour of their spear
Everybody knows they keep a machete in their back pockets
Do not go about asking for their political name
You will be breakfast, lunch and supper
To the pit bulls that keep safe their family throne
From daydreaming incumbents who think they have the political keys to Utopia, the land that doesn't bleed,
A land that shines on behalf of our black skin
A land where every bonafide African dreams of the throne as a possibility
I thought it wise to share the picture in a lyrical note….

A land where brothers share a smoke
Without the fear of what the other might spark with the flame thereof
The Hutu should not mistrust a Tutsi, that Rwanda is not what Africa desires
I think that world lies on the next political page

Only when the killer brothers denounce the bloody spear and the known machete
To embrace this light that makes my African skin visible

Shades of Black

Suppressed thoughts and burried dreams

Desires as nightmares, a life in quotes is whats faring

Revolutionary dreams dressed religiously
to spark the mineral loot

Starvation plays percussion while poverty plays the flute

They care less to see the nation bleed,

Their fiery eyes have seen the gore in war

When the pillars of the synagogue falls,
they blame the ground for taking too much from their hands

Their greed is the treasured end,
its consequences the music on our end
           Everything sour they say with their bitter tongues
We bounce to the taste

We stand deprived of our home
           Parrot poets preaching propaganda
to the walls around their masters-
                -All eyes on the gems

The glow and   glitter of diamonds is enough light in their lives
When we speak of darkness,
          we speak of a shadow whose reality they dont live
      Children bouncing to the West as the economy bounce to the
worst
Food for just the few and crumbs for the rest
Haven't we seen hunger from our mothers' wombs
The sting of its rays reflected
along the blàck of my skin
Haven't we tasted death from their assumed motherly boobs
A boulder by the roadside knows it;
They are the reason
the national flag forever weeps among the freedom flags of the
world

A serene breeze
  lures a roaming bird to the sea shore
    While a barren jungle scoffs the hunter
      We live to watch the nation drown
in the gore of its own citizens
because thats what the revolutionary gun spells
      We live to curse and rebuke
the reflections we get from the mirror
Because it was wrongly inscribed upon our lives-
Darkness comes to compliment the shades of our skin
        Pick a chunk to munch a bone
        and the day's struggle is gone
      We live the shadow whose reality exists in the foreign land
    Where my brothers and sisters live as foreigners
      Conforming to the shades of their skin colour

The Urchin in the Picture

Destiny is what provoked the wound on my face

We share the stink of a race this way thus

When they propose a toast of Champagne to happy moments

We have these salty tears to share for a beverage

The street is my home, out there it's never warm at all in winter

Our interaction with the sumner hail stones

Comes with no moderation of a roof above my head

Those people doing rounds in the city

Are the walls around me but they can only afford a pity

When none of them drop a rag in the bin
          I am all naked in the streets named after the revolutionaries

We hold those streets for a home
Many are the days we dine on tears in Robert Mugabe Street
To the tomb of the Legend, we ask Is that it
      The taste of freedom delivered to choke the living
   We sleep in the open expanse of Nelson Mandela Street
While the Zulu pull down the shacks of their brethren Bantu
      Before burning them with an exaggerated xenophobic flame
Lack is what provoked the migration to the Goli of Mandela
We burn in the embrace of Chinamano without an umbrella

Will these walls that birthed my ancestry
Give home to the homeless
The walls are not my home, i am the graffiti on street pavements
    The people are my hope,
What they spit, i pick and eat
What they trash, i pick and munch
    If they choose to drop a jacket, nights are warm with the jacket
for a blanket
I am the urchin who sleep in the open
    The providence of fate rendered me a life in those brackets

Letter To My Daughter

My heart is burning
From a flame ignited by your mother
I am not writing to put the blame on her
I am the proud one but truth knows family is about her,
How she put out the candle that shone in my face is testimony
Stacey my daughter; you were the songbird that sang the morning
songs i cared to listen to
Only you, knew how to strike the chord that could spark a sincere
smile on my face
You are that chord, no one else can define a melody to me

You are the flower rooted in my heart and mind,
The only flower that bears the colours of my life
I miss the said flower each passing hour
Nights come to haunt me for your whereabouts
I tried to recite those bedtime stories to poetry pages
Though you be the writer's daughter,
I have seen it with my life, you will never fit on pieces of paper
Beloved daughter;
When a flower rooted in the heart and mind is uprooted
What remains is a bleeding mind and wounded heart
I am walking alone to the newspaper stand and even the wind stares
at me in askance
I know that won't be good news to hear but that's exact where i
stand
In that bad....

Beloved daughter,
For you remain the seed of my groin-,
Take these my salty tears along the flow of this verse
There is nothing left to this miserable life i live

I am living a lie without you to tease me around
The world is bleak where the bleeding heart and mind promise to
take me
Beyond the taste of it all, i should have considered you for a bribe
Beloved daughter, for you remain the seed of my groin
You remain the flower i live to miss each passing hour
I am writing to admit that family is about your mother and myself as
father
You are my daughter as a flower and beloved KFD as your brother
Take these my salty tears,
Where i stand without you is a sure semblance of hell
E.D

Letter To My Son

Take these salty tears too,
My beloved son
I am groping in the darkness of days
Because of your absence my sun
You were the difference between day and night
| You were the blissful- end to each and all my living days
I have seen you crawl before me
And by the providence of fate i have seen you walk and run
I heard you murmur and by the providence of fate
I have lived to hear you say a word and talk
| No walk is a worthy walk if i do not walk with you-,
No talk is a worthy talk if i do not talk to you along the walk of life

I am reaching out to you
But my hand is falling short
The emotional distance between me and your mother falls outside
my arm's reach
You came to sweeten my insipid life
Is it ever easy to forget a taste to your life as long as you live
I see you in all my dreams-
We smile, we laugh, we cheer but that's not reality
When i call out your name
Tears roll down my cheeks to answer in your stead
Life is a stretch of dark without you my sun
I miss the stolen nights that began with your blessings;
'Good night daddy...'

Beloved son
You remain the treasured jewel of my heart
There was only one who knew the value of the jewel
I entrusted her with the keys to the safe

I am not writing to play the blame game here
Rather i am trying to show you what became of my life
When after the tragic storm, i woke up to a stripped heart that recalls
a jewel as yesteryear possession
I am going nowhere with this life
I shall say it until we someday walk together again
No walk is a worthy walk if i do not see you by my side
I take the blame when it comes from you;
I should have swallowed the grenade the way it came
Just so before it blew away our shared life as family
I am writing to admit that family is about your mother and myself as
father
You are my Sun and of course your beloved sister SHD
The worthy walk that is left for me is to trace the jewel and live the
day that comes with you son
I lost my heart to the hands that striped it off the jewel
There is no day in my life, i am living the dark
I miss you son, daddy loves you, E.D

Bhema Valley

Wherever there is a smoke,
They say there is a fire
All day they smoke,
They blame it on the political misgivings of their chosen legislators
Tomorrow the morning sun smiles on them
As they play hide and seek with the police
Who comes to share with them a rolled spliff
Before taking a bribe that okays the smoking
This is how the future bleeds in their hands,
This is how the future looks bleak in their eyes
Unless of course if you count the smoking for a worthy activity

Weed and codeine
Comes to answer their How questions;
How does one feature into the future's picture
That doesn't pose any hope tomorrow will be a better day
All day they smoke, watching their shadows of hope melt away with
the billow of their smoke
They smoke, they do not choke
This here is their reality, far from a mere joke
The graduates blame it on the police
Who chase them away from the streets
Where vending is the only end close to their desperation
The police watch the touts smoke in the streets
Verily they know it's not the touts who started the fire
The streets watch them pass around the spliff
All day they smoke, looking forward to the promised jobs,
Not the kinda odd ones which fuels the smoking

Bhema Valley, they will answer when you call unto them

They say it's the smoking that moderates their political rage

All day they smoke,
The tears they shed smoking have failed to put out the fire burning
their livelihoods

They blame it on the government
The government who blames sanctions for suffocating the economic
respiratory system

The said sanctions which put the blame on governance
This is how politics jeopardise their livelihoods,

This is how governance have rendered them political victims
They live forever high, above
what you say in undertones
        I see weed and codeine in their hands
In those hands the nation's future bleeds

Just how do you feed the famished children
When you chop off the hands that fix them a meal

Somebody ought to do something about the fire
Before the smoke chokes the nation dead

Tomorrow they will parade the burns before the parliament,
        Puke in their portfolios for watching the smoke defining their
living days

Tap of Cholera

Every street is a death trap
People walking on cholera to bask in the freedom sun
The look upon the streets poses to remind the residents how death
looms in their beloved ghetto
Streams of raw sewages flowing ceaselessly past their door steps
If it's not diarrhoea, it's typhoid
If it's not dysentery, it is the deadly cholera
Either ways residents scramble for a toilet seater
The wild grip of cholera is a sure way to the graveyard
By no surprise the gross smell of human waste
Is the air we breathe in the ghetto
The deadly disease is promised to us daily
By this unabated flow of sewages in the streets

Mountains of uncollected garbage at imposed dumping sites (sorry
The right word there is *Marabu*)
Speaks to tell a tale of a missing service
Surely the buzzing flies hum to question our sanity
Cholera took the life of a brother in 08
That was after the first run of harmonized elections
Remember how the cholera outbreak came to the residents of
Budiriro as post-election desert
The deadly disease took a neighbour's wife in '13
That was after the harmonised elections which dissolved the GNU
How the outbreak comes soon after elections remains a mystery
Fresh tomatoes here, grab a fruit paMai Juju,
Vendors pose as drivers after poverty drove them to the streets
When the vendors cry, they do not cry for cholera
They cry to shed a tear to a life of lack that comes after cholera
The relative bond between poverty and cholera remains confined in
the ghetto

Burst sewer pipes,
A sure sight in the ghetto
Streams of raw sewages flowing in the streets
Mounds of uncollected garbage at every breathing space in the ghetto
You ought to hear the buzzing flies hum to question our collective sanity
To understand how the residents are playing hide and seek with a promised death
Chlorinated water is not what the residents are asking for
We live with the tap of cholera, we see it everyday
Is there a known pair of hands mandated to oversee the closure of that tap
Death looms in the air we breathe,
It takes them an outbreak to wake up to the tap of cholera
By no surprise, the gross smell of human waste is the air we breathe in the ghetto

Beyond The Writer's Day and Page

Beyond the poetry page
Words exist to portray our image
Where we come from, where we are and where we are going,
Beyond the writer's day and page
The writer's wit continue to burn
And discard the stinking realities that choke and suffocate our
dreams and expectations
Verse is my game, i recite to invite the reader to a very page where
word is never served plain
Do not mistake me for a passer-by
I have come to resurrect and revive what the reader miss in
Marechera
I have come to answer the poetry questions that came beyond
Angelou's day

Beyond the writer's day and page
The writer's wit continue to illuminate the world of the living
Verse is my game, i recite to serve the meal of the day
This verse is about the justice that followed Marechera beyond his
grave
It's not for me to undermine the legendry's seductive penmanship
Justifiably so, the two of us were made out of the same image
Put the blame on me should you find that line offensive
Just do not mistake me for a passer-by
I have come to claim the space they left blank for a future verse
Flip over to the next verse should this one fail to suffice your
definition of verse

Wake up to the present,
I might not be there to deliver it on Christmas
Tell them all when they demand to know,

The bearded fella have come to ignite the literary flame,
The flame that scoffs and burn to ashes our ignorance and stupidity
Which continue to render us invisible on the global radar
I understand it's not easy to resist a verse like this
Tell me in literary currency
How much the living poets owe you in total
With this writing pen, i have come to settle the outstanding dues
Just please do not mistake me for a passer by
Verse is my game,
I have come to don the garments they deemed unfit for a Bohemian
writer
I am a counter culture that have come to breathe life unto fading
cultures
You can put the blame on me
If this verse has been such a mess
Beyond this writer's day and page
Word will continue to illuminate a world we leave behind
Until the ultimate demolition of confusion from man's psyche...
Meet me in the realm of light

Bowing to Kiss the Tomb of the Legend

Thy word is a serene rain
That pours to serenade the brain
The minute hand will not hold me back
When writers beat the drums with their pen
The clock ticking to hear the writers talk
Book pages blinking in a flip to witness how they wonk
Sapiosexuals getting intimate with the flow
Every literati is key to the chorus of the song

Verse is my hand,
Reaching the world to spell a name in that end
Book pages fade but word remains
footsteps of writers flowing with their ink
Let the thirsty reader confess after a sip
That lane is not mine to keep
I would rather flirt with the reader after a drink
See them like and share the intellectual dose of my ink
I have always roamed Harare as a geek
But i only care to deliver the fragrance, rhyme doesn't stink

I am the residue of what yesterday was
Word spells my essence, verse justifies my imminence
That way i am the shadow of the days to become
The legendary Marechera wrote the Mindblast
I live to pick the debris after the dust
He remains the sun shinning in galleries
Where a different kind of life goes on after the sunset
Awaiting dawn to spell another sunrise
When i bow to kiss the tomb of the legend
Thats only to confirm what my tongue is up to
If the truth be told;

I would wear Marechera for a garment
If it fits the reader before the mirror

Surprise Call

The day i came back home to find C.C gone
I did not cry, i lit up a cigarette and took a puff
I wanted to shout, i wanted to scream, i wanted to whisper
All at once i wanted to laugh
The first puff told me to forget about C.C and move on
The second puff reminded me
How it's never easy to forget the ones we love
The third puff advised me to listen to the cigarette
While the memories fade away with the billow
The fifth puff brought a picture of me and C.C sharing the same
pillow
At the crossroads of what to do
I called unto my sixth sense
Sleep on it. Sleep on it means taking the puzzle to the blanket
Where loneliness reigns in the absence of C.C and the kids

It's a lie, nothing fades with a billow of smoke
I see her face on every patch of ground around me
Smoke and booze only steals the troubles from the troubled
mind for safe keeping
When the beer departs the system
You wake up to the same passengers you tried to rid with the booze
I can forget the magic of her naked body at night
But missing her cat and mouse chase with the kids is
nothing alright

Tell me what to say
When the dirty dishes ask me what i think of the mess on them?

I never cried, but the subdued tear kept knocking
We danced to the song Isabella on her birthday
Me and C C, the two of us shamelessly -naked to the sweetness of
Kizomba
Who knows the songs she is dancing to in another man's arms
She closed the door to her loving heart
I watched her playing her part as planned
The reason i invited you in,
Where our love once bloomed like a flower
What exists between me and C.C
Are these poetry verses to fill in the spaces
She let be between the two of us
Who got that song Isabella on her music list
Like now i feel like dancing to the memories of what once were

I lit up a cigarette and slept on it
    I knew the subdued tear would find its way with the ripples of time
    I knew she would be back someday to check on me
Only i didn't know she would call on me this way
Getting to fit in my literary haven like an angel
        She had a world for me and she took that world with her
    I did not cry, i said fare thee well
When the love you seek cannot be found here
 Tell her i miss her though i might never care to see her again
If she asks of me, tell her i am now married to the cigarette
In case you didn't know;
That's how i became a chain smoker

Loving Lo

I fell twice for the same candy
I'm loving Lo; everything is on the go
She makes my world spin
I tell the loving heart living without her is a mortal sin
With just a smile, she sparks a life into my wretched heart
She, the same angel who gave me the taste of love
I made myself welcome again unto her loving arms
I am not reading much from the Old Testament
I am yearning to live with the new psalms and revelations she has
come to offer

Waking up to the same love
That faded with the black sun that brought untold darkness in my life
She remains the same flower that shines in my life every passing hour
She is the same flower that yesterday found the ruthless heals of my
wellingtons and looked less a flower to the eye
She is the same Lo that made me smile to the taste of love
She is the same candy stolen from me once by circumstances
The same Lo, the one and only sun that shines in my life

She is mine,
When she sparks the light to shine
She is mine when she remember still
How the two of us used to tango in love
She is forever mine if she can submit to my loving heart
Beautiful Lo is mine, everything about our love is as sweet as pine
Her love is my love,
The only love i have known and cherish
Now that i have seen what comes with the sunset
Her love has taught me that no other kind flies above our affection
Damn, yours truly the wordsmith can't seem to resist the seduction

I have seen and lived to believe the two of us are two matching
halves in love
Together thus we make the shape of love
I love you Lo,
E.D

Spelling My Flo

A good wind delivered the dose of love
  A known dimension of madness taking residence in me again
My mind is all subdued in the seduction of the dimples upon her
beauteous face
She admitted me in a special ward where the same is a reward
    The flower taking my heart for a fertile soil
    The bloom of her petals turning my psyche into a frenzy
She vowed to decorate
 my life with a scent of love
    Taking my life with her like a wave of death
I am dead in love because she is heaven
My soul smiles to the afterlife, a taste of heaven is here served in love
    Her pulchritude is a nemesis to what my heart can not resist
She settles it all with a smile that spells a different kind of love
When she said those words to me;
I looked back to pick up the shards of a loving heart
    Of course i love her too ,my heart beat to the music she sings
Love here is the religion ,
    I am living the madness behind in pursuit of heaven
She said repaint and love will be served
I took her arms for a brush, her loving heart for a new paint and the
two of us became in love
    Love is Flo, Flo is love ,i am in love with this Flo
      Damn, this sweet of a blonde punctuates my miserable life
with a spell of love

Here is to Flo Again

The truth can only be said in a whisper
From a distant i have envied Marechera for his Flo
But that envy is gone now, i have my own Flo
Black King , White queen
The pawns will move first ,i have a love to chase
Black and white ting, its just about the fling
Love coming to dispel the question of color prejudice
Its not like she is giving me a ring
We are flowing in love because fate wills(wheels) it
Maybe she is real, its hard to say
I took a sip, then another and another and another sip
I am drunk with a love that comes after the sip
Maybe She is real,
What matters is the Flo
The lines i write with her in mind
I think its true that love is blind
What I see through the poem are more than visions
Here is to Flo again

Blowing Wind

Word is my art
The art is a blowing wind
When the right wind blows, the dead leaves fall from a living branch
You can't blame the wind for blowing a dirty rag onto your door step
No, you can't hold anything against the blowing wind
When it brings before your face a stinking rag somebody else threw about
Writers only answer when their names are called
Their wit and lack thereof shines in poetry pages, words pointing to them as creatives
The reader gives a nod to what he finds sensible in the captions

Word is my art,
I'm the counter-culture that breathes life unto fading cultures
Look me up, I am the lyrical sculpture coming to add substance to existing structures
With this pen, I have come thus to relate how rendered circumstances of the day shall accompany us into a future awaiting
With this pen, I am justified as a lyrical directory to all that has been lost and seek to find
Justifiably so, I am the detailed map that doesn't shy to capture the shape and taste of our ignorance and stupidity

Word is my art, word is the serenity of human existence
You spark a smile when you serve it sweet,
You make them laugh when you capture the comedy in the streets
Honestly, how can you blame the blowing wind when it blows a dead rat into your dinner plate
Don't blame the wind for blowing a used condom unto the queen's cup of coffee

Do not blame the wind, everything it blows only comes as caption to
the flow of reality
What does it matter to pity the bleeding shadow when the object
exists before your eyes in agony
Language comes as bandage to the wound in a lyrical depiction
The native language lives in bondage, taken hostage in the very face
of cultural erosion
There, my name is justifiably called, I am the counter-culture that has
come to breathe life into fading cultures
How the blowing wind interacts with the present and the future,
I shall not say, I have already made a gesture

We Are Africa

We are Africa,
the land upon which our story is written
Africa the land, Africa the people -
Africa is the people and their land,
the spirit unseen that called us all into being
We are the embodiment of human existence,
The unmistakable drumbeat that resonates in the African wilderness
The sweet song their bitter tongues can't sing
We are the Bantu,
The two-toed Doma of Guruve who thrive on nature for their
sustenance
The Himba of Kunene, the Khoi Khoi and the San of Sossuvlei
We are the flowers of the Sahara and the Namib deserts
The flesh of the known, the spirit unseen that belongs
We are Africa

We are Ashanti, Balunda, Masai, Dinka
Rotse, Yoruba, Zulu, Tswana, Shona, Ndebele
We are the habitats of a land that tolerated black for a skin colour
We are the scars and traces of tears captured in poetry lines
We are the gold, we are not the glitter
We were neither buyers nor the sellers,
We were the auctioned slaves- the ware
The one in chains and never the bearers of the evil keys
We are the drops of blood squeezed from the African Kingdom
The blood that shamed Rhodes' somnambulistic colonial ambition
We are the flame of Marcus Garvey anti-slavery urge
The sum total of what Martin Luther dreamt of in America,
What Steve Biko and Walter Sisulu died for in Azania
What the people have always known and wanted

58

Spare me the narration that comes with human blindness,
The black they choose to see only satisfies the eye and the mind
which is blind
I'm putting it in braille so you get the jinx of it,
So your ignorance will not trespass my territory
We are the sweet song their bitter tongues cannot sing
We are the habitats of a land that tolerated black for a skin colour
We are the Kalahari flowers that beautifies the universe
We don't bleed black blood when the black skin is hurt
We are speaking to be heard because there is a better world known to
my being
We seek a better world where skin contrast is no drive to holocaust
We are the flesh of the known, the spirit unseen that lives

58

Peace On the Run

It was fun
basking in the new sun
The sting of its corroding rays
reminding us how yesterday came to pass
Hooray to the new days upon us,
Heads up held ;we stood with our dreams
Bitter days behind us, we rose to define the better
We donned the freedom on our faces to look the new
Chanting a taste of freedom for all to embrace
Dancing thus to the new rhythm
playing along to our anticipation of freedom

It was all to life,
an endearment as long as the freedom anthem plays on our turf
Washing our hands for an anticipated meal that comes with the hour
Tick tock , tick tock as we await the walk of freedom
One step turned an outright shock
The trusted brothers turned the muzzle against the people
That way we mastered the paradox of freedom in the face of greed
and power;
We discovered pythons from our own turf
They do not wail alone in Sudan,
The missing piece of freedoms in Khartoum
is a wound on thy beloved Africa
There is no fun in the new sun,
Peace in Africa is on the run
No spark of light in this rendered freedom
When we speak of freedom its only to observe the shadow
There is no serenity in this vicinity
Brutality and barbarity is their coined measure of civility

Brothers and sisters in the Dafoe cannot dance to the rumblings of war
That song is verily sore, that song cannot watch us fall
Popularised, politicised propaganda propagated to pollute the people
Politics perpetuating promiscuity to promote partisanship
There is no peace in Sudan;
The missing piece of freedoms is what the Africans long for

Greed and power turning everything sweet to sour
Gunshots the percussion to the civil wars playing across the turf
The dream of freedom remains in Mandela's prison bed
Freedom is amiss if you wake up from the delusional slumber
They hit the weak to keep the dripping tit to their lips
Those gunshots you hear are not merely to instill fear,
If they do not see their kin's blood its not politics
That way we mastered the paradox of freedom in the face of greed and power
We discovered pythons from our own turf
There is no peace in Sudan;
the missing piece of freedoms is what the Africans long for
There is no serenity in this vicinity
I rise to shame the bitter taste of such civility

April the 19th: A child is born Today

Word is my game
I am a counter-culture summoned by the justice of this realm
When i rise to sing a song, i don't summon the audience to a
dancefloor
I don't leave them hanging at a coma, rhyme after rhyme as i recite
I take them all the way to the full stop
When you see them dance to the verses in Breakfast with Marechera
that's just how they fell in love with the flow
Poetry between the lines
We are here to serve hope to the habitats of this House of Hunger
Ever wondered how this life we live resonates and fits in the lyrical
captions of Dambudzo the legend
This story is about how to claim the space, shame the rot on our
wretched face
And breathe hope and life into the avenues of existence

April the 19th, a child is born today
I propose a toast to the new sun that has come to shine upon our
creativity
It's a different independent story from that of yesterday; April the
18th
When the habitats woke up to a breakfast where bread
was a yesteryear narration in many homes
Drinking tears to the last memories of what their lives used to be
and how the Independence flame used to make them cheer to the
freedom flag
No bread on the table, the habitats of this House of Hunger were
excessively famished to go and listen to the village head deliver a
speech
Today we torch the Independence flame for the artists to articulate
with no hindrance

A guitar to the passionate guitarist, a piano to the pianist
The music in their fingers cannot die before their day is done
The Hub is our home,
We will be dropping bombshells of hope with intent to heal
For we have a voice to sing and question the social vices
We have bandages in abundance to heal the bleeding wounds
My word is a pill, serve me with a lyrical accompaniment of a mbira
and the world is healed
The Hub calls the painter to rise with his brush and paint the world
in humanity colours
Just state the price, as long as art is the currency
They are here with their creativity to pay the bill
Look no more for the lost poetry lines
For no poet can pose as the fixed cost of the craft
Look no further; this Hub is the directory towards the value of the
same
April the 19th, a child is born today
Let us together shout AHOY & ALUTA CONTINUA to this flame
we torch
Ahoy & Aluta Continua
Ahoy & Aluta Continua
Ahoy & Aluta Continua
Ahoy & Aluta Continua
I propose a toast to this dawn upon our creativity
Ahoy   and   Aluta   continua
*this poem was penned for the launch of the Mbira-Poetry Night, a weekly event
Dzonze curates at the Action Hub in Gazaland,Zimbabwe*

Peace in Pieces

Asuming my writing pen is pregnant with rhymes
The poet is here to settle the bill in rhythmic currency
Take me for a delegate presiding over this talk
 about peace
The geek is the seed
See them kiss and caress his thoughts on poetry pages
Holding dear what becomes of the writer's intercourse with reality
The fragrance of his words coming to define the taste of verse

Hell yeah; they serve bombs in food bowels
Preaching war in popularised propaganda
Prompting the said pepertrators to sip blood at will
Dust to dust ashes to ashes the deal is sealed
With the burial of the victim
Where is the love when
Gunshots is the hottest music playing in the streets
A love spelt in bloodshed,
Peace written off from the dashboard of humanity
In the absence of peace a life stinks like feces , Pooh
Give me a toast to a better world
Me for you, you for me and us for the world aint that everyone's cool
The world is burning from a blaze of war
The love for peace is the how to dowse the flame

We owe it to love for peace to reign
Love doesnt feign when all to peace we deign
Violence is the beginning to the end of peace
Peace is not peace when it comes in pieces
Where is the love
When protagonists are antagonised for their determination towards
peace

Wordsmiths rising to question the fall of a civilisation
Where is the love
When hate is the only music playing on the African turf
See the Bantu dance down to Xenophobia in Azania
Civil wars tearing Africa to pieces at the expense of peace
Bloody games going down in Africa
Calling thus the black of my skin to an unwarranted shame
Where is the love, when the question of peace goes unanswered

This Aint The Non Believer's Journey At All

Truth lies between the lines
The sweetness of the flow is not about how the picture tastes
| Rise to the vibe, it's how the writer's mind tastes
A writer knows how to capture the flow
We did not read Some kind of Wounds between the lines
We identify with the painted picture
Our beloved black skin lived with those kind of wounds
Greed and hate bore us the wounds
We said grace to convince the mind supper will be served anytime
soon
When supper time came we each said good night to the other
Sleeping on an empty belly
Because somebody unknown to me
Pulled some pages from Marechera's Mind blast to build us all this
House of Hunger
Where The Stone Virgins lost their chastity to gadabout politicians in
the wake of a new political dawn
Nobody saw the Coming of the Dry Season except Mungoshi

She No longer Weep is a word play dedicated to this House of Stone
She got impregnated with dirty politics
And when a child became of that unfortunate intimacy
Mr politician the father, reminded her how they had sex on Fools
Day so from the beginning it was a prank
The child was allowed to live forever after as a secret of these two
Of course corruption, is the politician's child
They roll our political will on ballot papers
Which they mean to torch and smoke to our political desires while
we renew our vows with poverty in disguise
Look where disguised hatred got us to
She sees this all the days of her life

Politicians taking the vulnerable for subjects their political disposal
get to punctuate
Who do you tell when you wake up to a Harvest of Thorns
And the Red Hills of Home tells you in a whisper....
Your hands drip of blood, yet your tongue doesn't know the taste of
honey
Come on board, modern politics is about money
Those are the Country Dawns and City lights my friend
That is Why She No longer Weep

We did not get to read Vera's Butterfly Burning at school
With our eyes we saw the Butterfly burning,
And when we tried to save the butterfly we got burnt
The scorching flame burned our fingers and for a while we could not
vote, nursing the burn
We Need New Names
When Batsirai Chigama rise to Gather the Children
Musayemura dropping lyrical explosives to shame the ills that have
come to haunt his kin in the Zimunya enclaves
We write to capture how the Queen's Royce rolls on the empty
bellies of famished urchins longing for just a day's meal
Where are you African Serenity
Where lies the path to the freedoms the writers don't seem to see
Xenophobia taking the Bantu for a meal out of misplaced wrath
I saw the picture in Chenjerai Hove's Up in Arms
The military getting militant to contain the civilians grief as opposed
to protest as a constitutional entitlement
I did not call those stories just to say hello to the reader
I rose to write so i ignite the missing light
Taking my story to a zenith where these voices shout to shape the
world
This aint the Non believer's journey at all
It's a continuation of where Marechera and Mungoshi

Left a line hanging, awaiting a weaver bird to weave the basket of
wisdom from their writing pen
I remember brother Olley telling me those words
This aint the non believers at all
I remember him saying while the two of us were getting lost to the
extreme confines of a liquor's embrace at Tazorora Tavern
I shout Freedom to rekindle
The lyrical dosage of Nyamubaya
This aint the non-believers journey at all

The Living and the Soar Song
A Poem written in solidarity with the victims of Cyclone Idai

Today we drink tears
in the cold embrace of a tragedy
Every tattooed descendant of Nehanda is soaked in tears
Breakfast, lunch and supper is not certain for my brethren in
Chimanimani
At the expedient behest of Idai, the unwelcome
who made himself welcome on the unsuspecting patches of home,
They drank and gulped bouts that sank them beyond the land of the
living
There is no remaining grain of hope in their granaries
to feed the survivors after a traumatizing wrestle with a cyclone that
left them naked
And if you think the clothes you give as relief aid will clothe them
from nakedness
You are looking at the wrong picture of nakedness
Their only shield from psychological trauma is our perception
They lost the serenity that defined their livelihoods
to a ragging storm, a cyclone....
A cyclone that became known to us as Idai

I call unto you again Nehanda
Pardon my misdemeanour around this, i got your number saved as
MEDIUM on my contact list
Say it to the African gods,
the very breast that suckles trees and crops for our sustenance
Is dripping venom, spitting out ceaselessly
to choke the living in their quest for a fresh breath
This land is flooded with tears of mourners
but we can't stand by and watch our actions drown the hope in the
face of survivors

Those who survived to live again
Today we share these tears as a narration of what befell our brethren
and kin in Chipinge
The wrath of fate delivered in excess, the damage too much a wound
for the human mind as to the skin
Yet we found it written as foreword that the living can only rise to
dance when fate sings a verse for us

Where was Noah to listen to Idai
prophesying the madness and evil intent of the cyclone
Dead bodies thrown around like teddy bears to provoke the pain of
the humane heart
Villages stripped of the serenity that made them home to our
acceptance of the same
Everything about life distorted, except the hope that lives after the
calamity
Life cannot be forgotten, we live to rise even after the cyclone
For time will tell a new tale to explain the graves
Today we share these tears to confront the providence of fate and
burry the pain to live again
The wrath of fate delivered in excess, the damage too much a wound
for the human mind as well the skin to bear
Today we drink tears in the cold embrace of tragedy as libation to the
African gods
Watching from the spiritual realms
Fate singing a soar song for us all to taste and dance to
For yours is a land soaked in tears today,
Take the horrible picture to the African gods Nehanda
The living cannot dance to that taste and remain with essence to
justify life

Fuck The Caption

When barbarity calls
The black brothers serve brutality in place of bread
Our tears for barbeque
Red blood, red wine what's the difference really in the face of this
barbarity calling
They take what their guns can deliver
Barbarity calls them to war
They call a brother foe to justify a fired bullet
Black brothers exchanging bitter words and vicious bullets to give the
world an episode of war...
I wonder what the black in them will say when confronted with a
poetry verse to rise to just one question;
What's the war about?

Blood oozing from the vein of political madness
Bullets and bombs sent to deliver the misplaced wrath
Killing the brother you verily know because war knows no brother
but enemy
Brothers are not the same when clad in the vile of politicized
madness
It's a civil war, a war among one black
Black brothers exchanging bitter words and vicious bombs to give
the world an episode of war
From the wars, heroes walk out with military honours and
decorations
Their children becoming masters at their fathers' game
Because they were told only our skin calls us brothers
Guns are not brothers, they were told to kill before you get killed
Africa is a shaping grave in their hands
At the end of their political reign we count graves for their
achievement

Where lies Africa in the civility of called wars
Where lies our common serenity in the context of civil wars
There is no civility in wars...

Shame this madness brewing Africa before you become the shame
Too much blood undermines our human worth
These "Civil Wars" are evil
Can't you see how they fail to honour our being
Guns got no eyes, but we should see the madness
What more can you expect the gun to show you other than
bloodshed
I am to you what you are to me because the two of us spells a being;
Africa
Can't you see how we collectively spell stupidity when we bow to the
call of gun
Fuck the caption coming to justify the madness
Civil wars is a measure of human barbarity

The Irony of Freedom

The wounds on my black skin
are taking forever long to heal,
Pardon me if i have the wrong prescription;
Is humanity not the pill to these ailments,
For how long shall we pay the medical bill in blood instalments?
The missionaries came with a burning light
That failed to illuminate the dark world only their eyes saw in Africa
Rather but sparked wars that sparked the mineral loot from dear
motherland

We housed the missionaries
and their hidden mission in our hospitable villages
They built bigger church buildings
that rendered the African traditional religion a quixotic nuisance in
the eyes of many who fell in love with their hymns
And they built a system that took us for hostages in our own turf
The "dark continent" became even darker
Only what made it dark was the disguised spark
And said of the African skin
the black you spell cannot bring any spark to the darkness we see
The darkness as seen, I mean the darkness that never was
We fought for our black freedom,
They broke the chain but remained with the key

They make us pay
for every piece of freedom that comes our way
We owe them nothing but they own the ways
Even this hard won independence did not come to stay...
They have got specified sanctions to punctuate us as subjects in their
political brackets
Yesterday they took my father for a slave,

Owned and sold him in a locked cage
Selling my tormented father in chains
To buy themselves material gains in plenty
With their political might
They take away the light to insurmountable heights
and if you are looking for fragments of truth on the polished surface,
It remains forever dark in the mind

They sing both the verse and the chorus
and task us to the dancing
That is why the wounds on my African face are taking forever long to
heal
We continue to say it in poetry verses
but they are quick to turn over to the next page
Silence the lines as quixotic, the poet's tongue as toxic
It's not like i am condoning that which they condemn
Rather i am condemning that which they have become-
The human gods of our humane world
Their haven is an earth size calico painted with human blood
When they kill they justify the killing and mock the deceased
Their judiciary whip is justified in their judicial dictates,
Its essence and imminence resonates with us
The wind that blows their flag blows the flags of the world
We cheer it when they preach the gospel
Its AMEN and AMEN to every Hallelujah they shout
We cheer it when they say it
Alas! They don't even mean the word
Everyone regrets it when they live the gospel they almost preached
extract from Edward Dzonze's poetry collection Breakfast With Marechera

The Black Hatred That Lives

When our collective madness unnoticed
Calls us all to sing and dance
I rise with my writing pen,
To sing a song of peace and dance to the real dictates of freedom
Detonating the ticking time bombs
Awaiting to swallow the children unborn
Because their fathers called a grave upon their wretched lives in a drunken slumber
The flame of their greed singing corruption as they dance to xenophobia in the absence of African serenity
When xenophobia plays in the streets
They bow down and thank the gods for the loot
What can the children say;
This xenophobia playing in their streets is older than their political scope

Black is my identity
I rise to its call, this Black is my serenity
Black is how i choose to go in chromatic justification
I know the dictates of the black i live, i know the sensation
I am the blackboard of white hatred and black barbarity, everything spelled in scars and bruises
My skin bears the scars of hate and love
I have come to give my story a wing so it flies like a dove
You might miss some captions if you choose to read it from the African flag
For the African flag flies silently in the wake of it all
What can it say to the wind that blows it back and forth in the direction of the flow
My eyes have seen what you will never capture from the colours of the African flag

When black hatred calls
The children cease to see the same black in another
They see only the call

They see only the call
Calling on them to unleash their wrath
They posed naked in front of a camera lens
When the flash came, they confronted the cameramen
For what his camera had seen of them
They took his clothes and asked him to take another shot
It just didn't seem fit for them to pose naked while the cameramen is
dressed
Together they looted, kicking a black brother they know because a
different song is playing
Looting, killing, burning the shacks that points at us as habitats
Stripping Ubuntuism in the very face of black existence
Saying when the people ask of this nakedness,
Tell them you were naked too

They met up with poverty and diarrhoea
Trying to pick up the serenity their fathers never bothered to honour
Because Aids and Ebola looked a picture too familiar to be discarded
from the African narration
The sun rose but forgot to shine
Blood was served as altar wine in called civil wars
The nationalists taught them the patriotism that lives
Underlining where the patriotism meets up with the corruption that
calls
When a new sun rose in their fathers' days
They were told to remember corruption and forget about patriotism
Thus to them a new word was spelt, nepotism
Nepotism told them thus;
A brother from just across the border

Should go back to Zimbabwe and sing Nora to the memories of a
missing plate for supper
They burned the Somalis, they tortured the children of Maiduguri
They removed the essence from the rainbow nation
Nepotism spelled to them as a gateway and not a limitation to their
capitalism
Nobody was allowed to ask where that path will take Africa
The only question they rose to answer being When is the baptism of
their children
In their eyes, every child of a nationalist need be born again
To see the god that comes with political power
Just live the sweet never mind who gets the sour
Saying heaven is a preservation of the few whose names are written
from the diaries of their fathers in politics
Forget about hell before you die
Africa is a haven for those who know how to trade the gold and pay
the tithe to their bank accounts
Before taking the dust to Rose the sweet teen
Her right hand takes the dust, while her naked body takes the AIDS
The day she got the virus, she pleaded with the corrupt minister
To please take my love for a thank you
Giving me a bursary does not go unnoticed
I looked at her, i looked at her befallen circumstances
The black hatred i saw lives not on her skin alone
The reason i am rising this writing pen to question our say towards
the same
The painted picture pointing at something coming to our existence as
caption

Memories of a Sour Reign

There is more to a stinking shadow
Than the missing object
They called us to a game
Had their say, touched our lives with their esteemed palms
When they depart from the picture
We had this poverty for a memento
They can't see the face of poverty
When it was upon them to shape a country
They distanced their existence from the proximity of rot
The face of poverty doesn't exist on their faces
Them here calls on all politicians
Who comes to mind when you look at the blood stains on the
African flag

The Way of Poetry

A life calls today the writer missed the call, poetry chose the way
the campus was always pointing in that direction
I lost my writing pen to the drunks in the bar
The cigarette became my pen ,smoke became my ink
sweet rhymes choke while the writer's life stinks
Word is on the rise, capped graduates rise to throw the dice
Academics will blush but i am not here for a word clash
This verse is an antidote for the wise,
Thats how the poet holds the keys to the gallery
Nobody sees the picture in his absence
Not that i am the all, my heart beats to the madness of the craft
The spook of the legendary Marechera lights up the way
My left hand holds what in art is right
My right hand holds what Marechera left behind
Darkness is cursed, a new light is called to spark the world
When that poetry calls, i will answer to remind the reader
Word was never buried , only the bones of the legends lie in pieces in
those tombs
Seek me no more in the avenues of doom
They have a vacant room for my poetry in America
The very taste of what they despised in Harare,
The only antidote awaited to save the world from the plague of
ignorance
When the drunks mumble to make an inquiry
Tell them a cool drink is brewing beyond the country's borders
The writer, all burnt in literature from the African sun
Goes after the ambrosia to sip and swim
In the literary taste of his fading dream
I could have chosen Madzimbabwe for Brooklyn
I care to write about the shadows of home in the African sun
My life is all burnt in literature from the same sun

Poetry could not endure the pain on pages
A life came calling, the writer missed the call
When he set to write a verse it was Adios to Harare
As the writer takes the way of poetry

As if Word is dead

Naked thoughts on decent pages
Distant realities mocking shadows of dead fantasies
Poetry accussing poets for their mediation to spare the vulgar from
biting a civilisation unnamed
Blank pages calling on poets to spell a civilisation
Shades of ink dressing people in decent clothes for what decency
should spell unto them
Readers getting intimate with the flow of poetry
Flipping pages to reflect and forget the stink on their skin
Summoning their ignorance , after consuming a rhetoric -to the bar
Where Marechera left a cigarette burning
Between the thighs of a bar lady
Who fell for his poetry
In the hope of saving the world from extinction
The cigarette burns on somebody's lips
Only the reader choose to observe the ash from burning pages
When the words unsaid ask for the decency of a civilisation
Nobody to assume the vulgar on paper
Graduates fanning the psyche with torn pages of Marechera's Mind
blast
Refusing to admit their mothers were the habitats of his House of
Hunger
Of course Mungoshi's departure left them Waiting for The Rain
I served Breakfast with Marechera- waiting could not be in vain

Black freedom bleeding on white pages
Only white forks can pick the wisdom to save their civilisation
Walking the passage of rite takes more than the dead
For the living are condemned to the genius of the dead
As if word is dead,
The spook of Dambudzo continue to light the way for the living
Because the rhetoric of the flow is mistaken for a metaphor

The Cock that Crows at Home

I know of a song
that we only sing because the lines comes to us without our effort
We sing poverty because that's what our leaders can afford to offer
We sing Xenophobia from an assumed hatred that sounds unfit to
spark a brawl
We sing Ebola, Cholera and Aids
Because nobody among us seem to have a pill
We sing protest songs, blazing guns playing percussions
Nobody likes the rhythm
Death echoes from the rumble of their drum beats
But from the devious look on their ugly faces
Killing is the rhythm of the season
the gunshots comes to remind the streets who own the   bleeding
town,
Who colours the pavements with human blood
and who gets to shed a tear when you call the brothers to your
attention

The cock that crows at home
captures the melody of our predicaments
When it crows in the morning
It's a reminder that the sun is up, poverty awaits the African, his
black skin the black board upon which suffering is caption
Black as the same, black as a colour code of starvation
Shooting continues in Bujumbura
More feared dead as Ebola takes our brothers in the Congo for a
meal
When it crows in the afternoon
It's to remind those on the payroll
that the price of fuel have gone up again
Bread, sugar and beer will be sold in US dollar

The price of pizza remains unknown to many
Who asks for pizza when just a bun and bottle of Coca-Cola
will turn your wallet inside out

We have stopped listening to RnB and Hip Hop
Gunshots comes at intervals, disrupting the flow of the music we
love to dance to
It's Thank you Sir, if you get your monthly salary in coins
These sounds are the pictures of what's going down the streets
When it crows in the evening
It's to say, you can sleep and dream
But the reality of those dreams is a nightmare
And the breaking news comes from the Avenues
If you are looking for a bit of jam jam to please the troubled soul
They have trebled up the charges
At least the money should buy her some cheese and a new pair of
undies
It doesn't crow in the night
because all our stinking predicaments seem to fall by the setting sun
yet to come still with the morning light
When your hear it crow in the morning
It's the same pitch to depict a known tone of our stinking
predicaments
When they pose for a picture in the newspaper
Their glittering faces doesn't reflect our befallen ills
Allow me in parting to say thus;
This poem is about the croak that calls the crow

Maybe My Name is not even a Name

I bought a sweet potato for the name
I took a bite, it didn't even taste the name
I tossed the sweet potato not at all sweet towards Fifi the dog
Fifi didn't even move, he yawned and tucked his head between his
limbs
As if to say, "You think i'm a dog?"
Mangoes are sweet but sweet doesn't accompany the name
Ask my tongue, honey, cinnamon and sugar assume the sweetest
What my tongue knows is what everybody smells with their nose in
this lyrical dose
The mind knows both the smell and the taste
I should not have bought a sweet potato
I should have asked before i pay a dime;
Where was honey, cinnamon and sugar
When this spud tasted sweet to earn the name
Only then i would have stood with a parameter
that spells sweet to the dictates
Sweet weighing sweet for sweet as a taste

Vultures and Vipers

They caged our rage
with bullets and guns
When they pee in our plates,
we bow down to the muzzle
Red blood, red wine
In the name of politics its all fine
A bullet to silence the protest and the job is done
Spit it or swallow the vile,
nobody knows who falls next on the line
Fresh bruises upon swollen scars
They called darkness into being
to become themselves stars by night

The doctor here is the witch
While we weep for dear motherland
They whip out the wit out of academics
to contaminate the flow of reality
Truth ,thus lives in exile,
Everybody wants to live awhile
Everybody to the lie,
A grain of rice to those who identify with their right
They have a life, we have a shadow
Adidas, Nike or Gorgio Armani pants ,
Dont be charmed by the tongue of the serpent
They suck the economy , they dont sip the blood
Blood is here shed as sacrifice to their political ego
O! Please dont mistake them for saints,
the vernomous serpents have their eyes inside your pants
Suck a life from the poor
before you show them the mirror ,
Give them to Dick for a penny because they are the poor

With the might of their gun,
they are quick to make a gambit
After nursing the wounds from their burns,
After mourning and burrying the victims they shot dead
Poverty, civil wars and brutality still in sight
And after all the walling to this pitied life
They remain the prophets behind the altar
Hell is my blackness have seen
Its either you bow down to their holly communion or you bow out
Red blood , red wine
in the name of politics its all fine
My beloved Africa suffers from the same ailment as yesterday
No medication, no cure
The doctor here is the witch

Cemetery of Mind

I'm not hungry anymore
I have become somebody's meal, i am only here to pay the bill
My life is up in smoke
I can hardly see the shadows of everything around me
Doom is nigh, i dream of Saints hungry for sex
Hot girls to burn my pants
It was this fame that sparked the flame
Ice cold ciders to drown and freeze the conscience
Hold on to the narration ;
The writer is damn lost to the beat his mind is dancing to
Every girl in a bikini is a new song worth dancing to
Love is a phantom of the poet's desire
Life is a cool ,as long as the shebeen queen
Keeps the ciders refrigerated

I'm hung over with a life like this
But please don't pass me the negatives
I believe in the only hope
Concealed in the next cigarette puff
If i don't live to see the billow rise to the sky
The rhymes will hang in my mind
And the reader will take me for murder
I don't want blood on my hands
I cast my lines in poetry verses
When the rhymes i write doesn't sell
I lit up a cigarette and walk this story
The hot girls burning me to a comma ,
Tuberculosis choking down the next rhyme unpenned
Ghonorea and Syphilis putting an endnote to a life like this
All i see in that cigarette billow is an epitaph
Harsh words awaiting a tombstone

To take residence after a life like this

Africa, To Whom It May Concern

Up and down the African streets in poetry verses
Dust is the majority, the gold is just a few
Purses are empty, prices are hefty
The haves are few, beggars are the majority
The cost of survival is forever going up
As I go further deep into deserted mine shafts
In search of a deserted fortune to keep up with the heights of fate
My sister's knickers drops down
As bread prices treble up
Selling her body to negotiate a meal for her impoverished family
The haves pay for it, not for the needy sister's sake
But for their own greed's sake

Beloved Africa
For how long shall you wear that gloomy face, For how long shall
you carry the poverty tag along with your name, For how long shall
we feed the hungry children With mere stories to feed their empty
bellies? Stories- Stories like once we had a spark before it turned this
dark Stories that never attempt to answer our only question; For how
long shall we live in this dark?

I refuse to lay low and spectate
While the radiance of my black skin
Is overshadowed by delusional trajectories sparked by greed
Beloved Africa,
You have got the land in plenty

I don't see how food prices are hefty
We've got dimples filled with gold upon our beautiful face
I don't understand how we are becoming a begging race
A blooming bosom of flora and fauna
There in the wilderness;
My fathers used to live in peace and harmony
Priceless curves that captures the eye with glitter
Bringing value to the body through its worth
I don't see how we are living poor with all the mineral wealth
We've got pendants of silver and copper
Dangled all over our body,
With the little drops of oil we have
Don't you think we can give the world
A healthy smiling face?

To be this black and alive
His limitless grace paid the price
To be such without pride;
Is closing our eyes in pretence of blindness
Dear Africa; it is you to whom it may concern
To conquer the darkness of days
All we need is a glow of light
Not the light from a fired bullet or a firefly
Rather we need lights in the African streets,
A light that sparks a sincere smile in every African home
A light that forever shines,
A light that shames darkness from our African homes
A light that illuminates the African spirituality
To awaken African pride in the conscience of all
A glow of light that shames corruption
A light that makes me visible,
A light that justifies our human worthy
A light that lasts the span of life…

To that end I proclaim my love for black

African Sunset: How Their Choices Makes Our Word Bleak

Hate is what makes the African world bleak
Hate amongst one black
Black brothers in parliament who bow down before their ego
The African flag is up in flames
The gun shots we hear everyday do not come to solve a thing
What does it matter to count the dead bodies in the streets
Remember the gun shots only come to confirm anew our fears,
There will be more bloodshed in Kinshasa
if the rebels doesn't submit their rebellion to the government of the
day

Politics is their game, even the gun is not to blame
Who cares who gets hurt, nobody lives with the shame
When it happens to my Africa it doesn't happen to them
The Africa i speak of is a victim of their political manipulation
I speak of a brutalized Africa that is tired of their brutality,
I speak of an intimidated Africa that is tired of their intimidation
I speak of a tormented Africa that is tired of their barbarity,
I speak of a divided Africa that is tired of their hatred and greed;
Packaged premeditated propaganda purposefully polished and
prescribed
to the people to pursue the same political poison
served on the political altar as holy communion to the grieving
streets
Do not bother to open the Bible
they have got poetry lines that pleases the politician and save the
parroting poet from the stinking prison

Where are you Addis Ababa, the land of our dreams
What happened to the African sun that shamed
suppression and oppression in the wake of colonialism
This one is for you Nyerere and Kaunda-
You saw the dawn, you both saw the sunrise
Rebellion and sanctioned protests the new world order in Africa,
Is rebellion the cause of the tragedy in the Darfur, Kigali and
Yaoundé
Show me where from comes your bloody tears Mogadishu,
Maiduguri and Kampala
I saw the political reign of Mugabe the nonagenarian
He saw the sunrise, he lived the brighter days and he saw the sunset
Tell it to Africa, Mugabe
Is it about the land or the bejewelled political end,
Tell me who sips the blood of all the political victims we continue to
bury on the African turf

Mandela and Kwame Nkrumah wanted the United States of Africa,
Is that it, Kenyatta...
We saw them terrorize Gaddafi on our own backyard
I watched in tears the American soldiers
taking the African flag for a mop to wipe away the dirty African
blood
that made their American eyes itch and sore
Not that i sympathize with the grave of Gaddafi
or his unsanctioned thirst for human blood as they saw it
With these my eyes i have seen and tasted xenophobia,
My father survived Gukurahundi and still got scars to show for the
tragedy
I don't know if my sisters are still alive with the Boko Haram
extremists
In all this, i sympathize with the fate of the African blood

Politics being their game, even the gun is not to blame
Sprouting civil wars the immediate measure to our African
civilization
Who cares who gets hurt, nobody lives with the shame
When it happens to my beloved Africa it doesn't happen to them

Let the poem breathe life into our shared madness,
Let it bleed for the wounds we can't contain,
let it bleed and shed a tear if the people can't attach the madness to
the blackness of their being
Let the black brothers in parliament play loud some jazz music in
their trendy Merc
if that goes along with the colour of their world
I will be singing songs like these from the African corridors
until their official mandate finally gets to meet our befallen
predicaments in the streets
Surely the sound of a fired bullet is not the music we desire
Please don't take much from their skin colour, it's never about Africa
when they fart in public
They can make peace reign if they can observe the African flag
before they choose to honour their greed
The warring flame marauding the African flag is a choice they made
on our behalf,
They could have stamped out the cigarette stub after a royal smoke
but they chose instead to watch it live to spark a flame
a ferocious flame that grows beyond their political heights
Unfathomably so, what peace only demands of them is just a political
will
It's for them to strike a chord and for us all to dance accordingly
They can choose to make the wound heal
but it's never their blood that's how peace is never in their minds
We want them to silence the gun shots
With their right hand they motion the military to get militant

yet still their left questions the flow of the drama
Watching through the window, innocent citizens running away from
a fired bullet

Diplomatic Call

There is a mist on the throne,
everybody wants the dawn and not the beast
The streets choke, the nation bleeds
when the African gods deliver their wrath in a strange tone
The different songs we sing to dispel the wounds on our skin have
got no audience
Nobody cares what the song says, nobody cares how much gets into
the neighbour's plate
as long the bigger chunk falls in their own
It's not the wailing but the gunshots
that compromise the next sunrise after this day is done,
Sing the song for us all Cabela
Do not take what is left of Kisangani
after the bloody confrontation with the deadly Ebola
Nobody wants the war,
Nobody wants the fall
Give us a signal of peace before you go

The African flag is up in flames,
set ablaze by those who vowed to serve and protect the will of the
people
Political madness haunts the people, people live with the madness
Politicians use politics to civilize the people ,
They perceive the government eye as holy
and everything antithetical as evil
Sing the song for us all Cabela
You know what's holly, you know what's evil
Save the piece of the African flag in your hands from the scorching
flame
Nobody wants the war,
Nobody wants the fall

Show us the dance of peace
when you are called to dance

It's the mist on the throne that provokes me
how can i remain silent when all i know about African governance is
violence...
It's not for me to point to the beast
for i know not in what direction the anticipated dawn shall come,
I might not have read the genesis
but the blackness of my own skin have not been spared by the
nemesis
Sing for us all Cabela, a song
that heals the political wounds upon Kinshasa
Before we could silence the rebels,
let the Addis Ababa parliament silence rebellion from the African
turf,
Before politicized madness could silence the poets of truth from
reciting
let the African parliament sing a song against war, take governance to
answer the how
I am counting on you Cabela,
I know you can silence the gun
before the sun goes down on your reign
Nobody wants the war,
Nobody wanna see the Christmas lights from a fired bullet,
Now that you know the song, strike the gong
Save the piece of the African flag in your hands from the scorching
flame

Made of Black

Some,
Not accustomed to my mental strength,
Say to me;
You were brutalized and terrorized
Humiliated and traumatized
Yet you smile and speak with dignity,
You walk like a dignified giant-
So I say to them:
I am made of black
To walk past experiences,
I am not vilified by history
I have a story of my own to write,
Battles of my own to fight
I am gratified to live for humanity.

Some,
Not quite accustomed to my contentedness,
Often demand to know
The indefatigable drive behind my composure
And so i tell them with a composed voice;
I am civilized enough within
To appreciate and respect creation
As long as I live
And to fear only the creator
I go for civility ahead of stupidity
That; if you ask me
Is my understanding of humility
Oh! Yes indeed I'm gratified to strive for humanity.

Some,

In utter askance at my stature
   Get it straight from me
Before they motion for it by word of mouth;
I am made of black to exist
With pride, made this way to subsist.
Celebrated in the myth of creation,
This life taught me
To regard another as an equal creation
That's what makes me
Smile and laugh off the stupidity of racism,
That's what inspire me to live on
As you can sure see…
I am gratified to live for humanity.

The Politician and the Povo: How the Music plays in the Zoo

We were told it's a taboo;
everybody bows down when the king wants to pee
Who knows if they sell it as bottled water in the streets
It's true there is a line in this poem that gets the reader sick
Nobody sells bottled pee disguised as spring water
but some of their cheap slogans does that
Never mind the who is who in the picture,
this is how the music plays in the zoo

Forget the who is who,
meet the cast along with the crew
The drama unfolding here is the chorus of the song;
Certified academics salivating for the politics of the land for its
bejewelled end
the unsuspecting electorate cheering to the President's cry for peace
as the 'boys' take the same for the signal to drop the explosive
that became an end note to the sermon of the day
Blowing to pieces the essence of the sermon on the very pulpit where
peace was preached
the smoke choked both the politician and the povo indiscriminately
before we took the peace home,
we took our injured friends to the nearest hospital
I took the peace home, the explosive took the life of a friend
I took the peace home, politics took the other piece of me

Forget the sound of the explosive if you can,
the voice of the deceased will forever echo in this penned verse
Politics is the shared face
if it's not partisan politics it's politicians practicing dirty politics
and either ways it's not easy to tell apart the crook from the spook
We are the bait on the political hook

Terror and brutality no better than xenophobia,
the vilified measure of African barbarity
I chose to capture the verse
to shame the brutal scars on my beloved face
I chose this lyrical flow for the chorus
to dispel the tainted tag pinned on my beloved race
If you were never told, it's a taboo
line two is just a rhetoric, don't take me for perfidy
It's true; there is a line in this poetry verse that gets the reader sick...
I lost a friend to an explosive that missed the president at a star rally

A Cry for Peace

This hatred
i so much condemn,
is man's worst form of relating.
If hate is the only food on the menu,
I'm holding onto my appetite;
suppress the crave until they cook it right
Paint the streets with tears and blood
Assuming humanity is not colour blind,
I want to see them walk those streets by day...
i want them to remember the gore.

This hate
i truthfully condemn,
Cannot be a sound track to our evolution.
Hate runs parallel to peace,
it is a muscle to man's concupiscence.
If hate is the only beverage in the bar,
I'm holding on to my thirst,
suppress the crave for the meanwhile
reciting lines and verses that question our sanity,
rhythms and rhymes that expose us to our stupidity.
Assuming we still have the conscience
I want to see them meet the hatred in the streets...
i want them to know how we so much yearn for peace.

We see them hug on t.v
but we don't feel the love in the streets,
We see them kiss and caress
but we don't quite feel the affection.
What's there to embrace
when we see them enjoy the smoke

while a flame is burning to ashes
the face of humanity?
We want to see them rise to the brutality
cease the killings in the streets,
end the terrorism in the world.
We want to see them rise to the barbarism,
end the wars and settle for peace...
We want to see them rise to the tide.

Living Black, Loving Black

Evolution is the rhythm of existence
Evolution and existence is the essence
The question of color is utter nonsense
Wisdom is the wit to resurrect the intellect
through lyrical connections of deep meditation
Knowledge is light, wisdom is the glow
I chose to write, i chose to recite
Only i did not choose this flow
It's like some stories tell their story
While we listen to pass and share the taste
What we were come to pass,
We reflect, we connect, we learn and only get wiser if we understand
Only if we understand...

       Let me ask;
Are we not the story to be told
We the tellers of that story because we live the black they see
     What they perceive of black is a reflection of what we give
To give the story a glow,
      Are we not the ones to flow
Pitch black, as dark my skin could be
       Truth is always in sight
You only need some light to get inclined to the heights
    I am forever unapologetic for my black skin,
     Black being and the black they chose to see in me
     My skin is the dashboard of black narratives undiluted
    I am the story of black, the teller of that story
   Only apologetic for holding on to my story
OH, yes if it pleases to hear i am sorry

Whose children are these

Hoisting in vain a flag of rags
In pursuit of a being, through ancestry the human mould could not
befit of them
Truth is always in sight;
They are the black story of the story of black
They chose to trade the melanin pristine
For a chemically negotiated lighter appearance
The world is a bliss of dark by night
Ignorance is their light, they will never get it right;
Black calls in our African-stead only as a color
If you care to know...
Black defines the appearance
Yet we moderate and justify the being to our taste
Identity is the essence, prejudice is utter nonsense

Winking in Ink

Can i please take you on a poetry date
Rhyme is my fate, verse is my face
Kiss and carress the here and now
Of word in the lyrical space
Dance to it in rememberance of Dambudzo the late
This ink is called to tame
The old face of the new world
In lyrical justice
Sapiosexuality is my offense
Committed to the crime to make the poetry sense
Tap and lick to the glow of word
I live the skint in literary pants
Nonetheless a passionate adherent to the same
When my day is done
Book pages shall recall my name for the stink

A Dance in the Dark

I see shadows dancing beneath my pillow

Motioning for a cigarette between my lips, smiling for just the billow

The music plays from a distant,

Menacing silence playing to the rhythm of horroscope

The distance between silence and a distant thought of what music could be in this embrace

Tears flow, yet a smile nods to the music

Darkness itself churning rhymes that glides along the flow of tear

Nobody dares wipe away the tears lest the music comes to a halt

Because those shadows are not alone on the dancefloor

The song sounds familiar ,only the dance is strange

The faces of those shadows are not at all strange

Only the thought of them being shadows is perplexing

Naked bodies dancing for a pair of knickers

The audience lusting for what they cant have

Its the music of the dead they are dancing to

Through the window, the dance looks bizzare

Its only when one of them pees in your cup

That you wake up from the dancing shadows

Where this music plays

Nobody gives a damn who drowns in the sewer

Even when they know they are sh*****g on the table

How everybody is dancing beneath the mask is not a fable

Like the morning dew, everything melts away with rising sun

The music doesnt die, it subsides into an echoe

That soon becomes a new song awaited for long

Even when we dance, nobody rise to match with those distant
shadows

Now buried in the realms
Where fate will bury us someday
®

Mmap New African Poets Series

If you have enjoyed *Shades of Black* consider these other fine books in **New African Poets Series** from *Mwanaka Media and Publishing:*

I Threw a Star in a Wine Glass by Fethi Sassi
Best New African Poets 2017 Anthology by Tendai R Mwanaka and Daniel Da Purificacao
Logbook Written by a Drifter by Tendai Rinos Mwanaka
Mad Bob Republic: Bloodlines, Bile and a Crying Child by Tendai Rinos Mwanaka
Zimbolicious Poetry Vol 1 by Tendai R Mwanaka and Edward Dzonze
Zimbolicious: An Anthology of Zimbabwean Literature and Arts, Vol 3 by Tendai Mwanaka
Under The Steel Yoke by Jabulani Mzinyathi
Fly in a Beehive by Thato Tshukudu
Bounding for Light by Richard Mbuthia
Sentiments by Jackson Matimba
Best New African Poets 2018 Anthology by Tendai R Mwanaka and Nsah Mala
Words That Matter by Gerry Sikazwe
The Ungendered by Delia Watterson
Ghetto Symphony by Mandla Mavolwane
Sky for a Foreign Bird by Fethi Sassi
A Portrait of Defiance by Tendai Rinos Mwanaka
When Escape Becomes the only Lover by Tendai R Mwanaka
وِيَسهَرُ اللَّيلُ عَلَى شَفَتي...وَالغَمَام by Fethi Sassi
A Letter to the President by Mbizo Chirasha
Righteous Indignation by Jabulani Mzinyathi:
Blooming Cactus By Mikateko Mbambo
Rhythm of Life by Olivia Ngozi Osouha
Travellers Gather Dust and Lust by Gabriel Awuah Mainoo

Soon to be released

Of Bloom Smoke by Abigail George
Denga reshiri yokunze kwenyika by Fethi Sassi
Chitungwiza Mushamukuru: An Anthology from Zimbabwe's Biggest Ghetto Town by Tendai Rinos Mwanaka
Because Sadness is Beautiful? by Tanaka Chidora
Poems of Risistence by John Eppel
Shades of Black by Edward Dzonze

https://facebook.com/MwanakaMediaAndPublishing/

Printed in the United States
by Bookmasters

Printed in the United States
By Bookmasters